BLACK LIQUOR
Dennis E. Bolen

OTHER BOOKS BY DENNIS E. BOLEN

Stupid Crimes | Anvil Press, 1992
Stand in Hell | Random House, 1995
Krekshuns | Random House, 1997
Gas Tank & Other Stories | Anvil Press, 1998
Toy Gun | Anvil Press, 2005
Kaspoit! | Anvil Press, 2009
Anticipated Results | Arsenal Pulp Press, 2011

BLACK LIQUOR

poems

DENNIS E. BOLEN

01 02 03 04 05 06 18 17 16 15 14 13

Caitlin Press Inc.
8100 Alderwood Road,
Halfmoon Bay, BC v0n 1y1
www.caitlin-press.com

Text design by Kathleen Fraser.
Cover design by Vici Johnstone.
Cover image, "Sawmill at the Greensboro Lumber Co., Greensboro, Ga. c. 1941," by Jack Delano, Library of Congress, Farm Security Administration—Office of War Information Collection 11671-10 (DLC) 93845501, call number LC-USF35-261.
Edited by George Payerle.
Printed in Canada.

Caitlin Press Inc. acknowledges financial support from the Government of Canada through the Canada Book Fund and the Canada Council for the Arts, and from the Province of British Columbia through the British Columbia Arts Council and the Book Publisher's Tax Credit.

Canada Council   Conseil des Arts
for the Arts   du Canada

BRITISH COLUMBIA
ARTS COUNCIL
An agency of the Province of British Columbia

Library and Archives Canada Cataloguing in Publication
Bolen, Dennis E. (Dennis Edward), 1953–, author
    Black liquor / Dennis E. Bolen.

Poems.
ISBN 978-1-927575-24-6 (pbk.)

    I. Title.

PS8553.O4755B53 2013   C811'.54   C2013-905059-0

for Janet Finlayson

black liquor, *a & n.* **1.** *by-product of the kraft process; cellulose breakdown;* **2.** *toxic water/alkali soluble degradation components containing more than half the energy content of the wood;* **3.** *carbon-neutral renewable source for industrial power generation;* **4.** *potable hydrocarbon infusion of organic molecules such as acetone, acetaldehyde, tannins and furfural;* **5.** *sugar cane distillate with specific gravity less than 0.91984;* **6.** *containing more alcohol than proof spirit (greater than 49.3 per cent by weight of alcohol) (colloq.);* **7.** *dark rum;* **8.** *bile and/or body humour associated with foul temper; slang* [late OE **blaecce likker**]

CONTENTS

GROWING UP INDUSTRIAL...

EVERYBODY

Everybody knew somebody

    Age of battered pickup
    cigarette load ashtray butt

Everybody knew

    grease coif armpit stain
    snagglepick match tooth

    Beyond
only the responsibly parented survive...

Everybody knew beltless toddler

Everybody

    Unrestrain seat bench projectile
    to the outskirts of wisdom

    Everybody knew somebody dead
    of car wreck

      Undershirt men
      cross-eye sway fatigue
      pace toward a next shift
      to hew and draw and maintain
    skirted metal house with wheels
    rented concrete

    Smoke death and like it

everybody knew

to cull those lucky not otherwise demised
of proud ignorance

Everybody knew

    none should crave education
    Drop out by 16 or you're not a man

Everybody knew

    alcoholic
    frown drink burp asleep
    door-slam solitary

Everybody knew men curse pregnant women

Weep
Shout
Things broken

        When the truck flies everybody off the road
        swat the kid who won't shut up
        fiddle the dial radio
        Leaden sad song
        soon silence

MR RAGE

In 1964 we heard a ranting war vet
temperament an unreported casualty
not twenty years out of the fight zone
A fearsome thing for a child to face
Hell we were only in Grade Six

He was a kind man mostly and knowledgeable
preferred teacher if you wanted to know

    combat stories and blood
    death and messy suffering
    and how likely it was
    Yes, he said, *absolutely for sure*
    based on his red-tinged perspective
    and read of contemporary times
    and gauge for the Cold War
    and bruise blue human cruelty
    More than a statistical trend
    A damned certainty you kids!

That someday we would be at history's displeasure
like him
    Ragged and enflamed

    a haunted house on lurching legs
    Anger spume from every window
    Spin bats in harsh daylight
    Dank room in which no-one will go

TOUGH

There was a fellow maddened
oversize
grades ahead
who for some reason went asking for hurt
A punch in the stomach
Right here, I dare ya
No way we said
You'll fold to jelly
We'll get in trouble
No way he said
I got steel guts
Been exercisin' tough

So everyone
big or small or timid
took him
on this invitation
to free infliction
of some TV imagistic manoeuver
Ignoring the dishonesty
of doing upon another
that which we would dread having done to us
We instead self-pictured
as dramatic stars in our own fight scene

Cutting knuckle to abs
rattle wrist to arm
Jolt sore to ache
in the spirit of schoolboyism
none of us dared whine
At least not there in the field of play

But he was such a rock
never so much as an undulation
no jack-knife slightly forward
Each boy-jack of us aghast
at such super-staunch stolidity

The legend of Tough went town-wide
and we all slugged away
with or without invitation

Then our war-vet teacher
     principal and gruelling historian
     appeared one day stepping livid
     Grabbed two boys punching
instructed punchee to follow
     Marched the coterie into his secret unseen
     mysterious office
     where for an hour low talking was not quite heard

Then to our desks came loudness
impact
Two for each hand
The first eight near lost amid whimper
The last four unaccompanied

     leather-on-hand
     our seized breath
     harrowed psyches
strain

to withstand the aural
the tactile and near olfactory
aspects
of our witnessing

          And the next day
     when the sore boys came to school
     their hands red-tender and lightly used
     the tough boy remained stoic
     Though he never did the stunt again
     in fact, scarcely spoke ...

The point of all this being
he and the principal ended friends

          A few weeks later
     on the day we last saw him
     I was outside clapping the chalk
     from blackboard erasers
     and through the grit-white cloud about me
     saw off by the road
     them shake hands

               And Tough walk away
               No books
               No bag

          A rumour passed that at age not quite fourteen
          without having finished Grade Seven
          Tough was working on a road crew

Decades later
walking my walk
bearing briefcase and badge
          I thought I saw him press weights
                    with tattooed determination
                         across a federal prison yard

          but never having known his proper name

          could not be sure

PLAY

The kid flying rubber-band
balsa toy airplane
afternoon hours in the street

Kitchen window Mom smile
at little boy's intense toss and run
wary of the lumbering

deco-sculpt auto masses
floating by singular once in a while
(traffic in 1960 never heavy)

The gentle roll-past
      family men at the wheel
      returning besuited
      wearied by productive days
      caution in slow down
      reverence for everyone's progeny

While sonny twirls the prop
and with narrowed seriousness
plans the path of a numberless
trip in the air about him

      And when not aviating
      scours ditches and unbuilt lots
      for sun-solidified mud clumps
      to hurl TV grenades

and seek that ultimate dust-puff
ersatz explosion we create
in our eight-year-old souls
when playing true

THE BEACH

June tide-surf cold
hip-deep ten-year-olds in a line
watch teacher demonstrate
Australian crawl

      roll of head and chin
      snatched breath
      fearless immersion
      And repeat

Wondrous value in learning
skill to last and save
      a lifetime

The crux of that day
      and several like it

         Cruel cold through every sinew
         weeping frigid
         peeling quick and frightened
         that life might not come back

But then wet swim trunks wave
side mirror
radio antenna

      When play is left upon sand
      bed beckons
      the half-hour we arrive home
      After a bath and the rubble between toes
      slip down the drain
      sluice home

Stinky seaweed dream
eternal sand chafe
    languid rise off sun-baked road

ROOT BEER

Craving ice milk products

     I made unwise friendship choices

Knock-around kid named Gordy
lived overtop the town diner

     seemed intent to keep me around

with the frequent bribe of a chocolate-covered treat
or ice-cream float

     Root beer was my favourite

     We'd ride bikes
     Go to the beach
     Caddy over aboriginal golf ground

where skulls were unearthed yearly
by schoolboys oblivious
to ancient strife

          the otherwise placid environs
          Qualicum Beach Country Club

Frequent rich mostly Americans
among whom I felt smally special
and once ferried the gear of a regal woman
who stated to her partner things like:
I met a mahhn in Vegasss
who knew your faaatha very well…

And I who as junior club member
of one evening in a twosome
sat down on the ninth hole bench waiting
with Fred Astaire and Bing Crosby
after Bob Hope apologized to me
for losing his ball and let us play through

And amid all this glorious legend

      we frolicked in the surf and searched the roughs and gullies
for lost balls the pro would pay us fifteen cents each
enough for a chocolate bar or frozen treat and some
left over for a down payment on another one…

    Into this idyll
Gordy whips one day
a felt-lined case
under my face

Look at this
Uh huh
Cool eh?
Uh huh

I had wondered
    when shown the sanctum above the diner
why it was that a mother and a son
existed in a place solely of leather couchwear
unused kitchen (I guessed they ate downstairs)
and a different fellow each time I saw

    But not half as much as I puzzled
        What were the glass and metal implements
nestled in the fitted interior
    of Gordy's new treasured possession?

That was the summer we moved away
        Just in time perhaps
                It would be years before I learned
                        what grief in the wrong hands
                                a hypodermic syringe
                                could wreak

FIRE IN GENERAL MONEY PARK

They saw help was needed
comic
when he ran for the bucket

Flaming garbage hamlet grass
pungent
railside vegi-detritus

that was good to burn down
often
to discourage rats

Nine years old with eager ignition
permission
At ten a pyro-weed expertise

but a Qualicum gust ambushed as it tipped
sailboats
in the broad bay

The day he set General Money Park afire
hands
of those who came

to sweep fronds of expert broom
whip
yellow flower fling to air and dust

Flame-out instant swing stroke
firemen
Solemn dutiful heroic

The notion of an off-duty towhead
paperboy's
possible descent into fume and flame

an affront perhaps to their universal
cohesive
mental containment

beach town's golf streetlight
freedom
and other reasons not to leave

CHURCH EARLY 1965

Altar boy *mea culpa* mutter
    Sacred age
    Sacred night and day

Robed to span the historic *saeculorum*
    between *Opus Deo*
    and schoolboy mental strains of

        The Beatles

Priest and help minister the chapel gloom
    Two lone ladies of devout face
    pray into the consumptive quiet

We four sing the ancient diction
    to all who do not hear
    will never be

        Were

and are not now

THE ARIA OF JACK

Opera entered life via shop class
crusty Italo-Brit motor genius Jack
who
while having us tear down engine blocks
change tractor oil
might curtly cuff a down-bound miscreant

>Fist reputation
>a solid
>apparent remedy
>for any problem one might have
>in institution or in life

From the mouths of those who knew
if any teen-boy of us stepped off-line
or lipped the short man from Manchester...

>*Jack'll hit 'im once*
>said my pal Glenn
>who had not long before
>done that
>and finished that way

>And whose air war experience...
>Burma nearly killed him as it did his friends
>DC-3s bounced off runways
>dysentery jungle dirt
>and the first jet plane
>whine thunder of anger and design

At assembly over Xmas
after we'd played our suite in brass and woodwind
Drama had stepped through their Yuletide skit

Lights dim and curtain draw
Nessun Dorma Jack on a bare stage
confound me
and in three minutes of vocal *non sequitur*
rafters resonant
turned me from confused to quester
ever since toting books
urbanized and in the run
to ably pretend
seek *biglietti La Scala*...

fit in even less
For lack of Jack's fist skill
to the life I left
scarcely think about anymore
except when I see a jet fly and the flame of its roar
is the aria of Jack

TO THE 1969 AMBULANCE

What was the flame panic
the efficient terror
flicker light sweep
down dirtside milltown thoroughfare?

But all was soon known of course
a boy head-on and his sister
de-limbed aboard a motorcycle
girl a schoolmate of mine

Who'd turned to me in class not a week prior
inquired after my closed off girlfriend
how long we were and why now were not
Did I hear clear what she asked me?

In a burg of non-exception working work
toilsome industry father
aborted school term
apathy-tuned paycheque reception

Struck to watch the medevac lights-off slow
short of the hospital
They do that the industrial men said
When somebody dies in the ambulance...

Slow down and take time not to kill anybody else
Consider the moment of the sky and life
Stop pulling lumber and paper kraft
wipe a face and scan community headline

Could I have saved her life?
Run and asked the time or a dollar or a date
halted for a second the driveway revs
made Fate dis-align a swerve second?

Next day as the mills wrung black liquor
say again ambulance
Was there audio to emergency ears?
Anything told? Hear clear what she asked me?

GREENCHAIN CANTICLE

Out aside the tarmac
under breezeway shingles huff
shoulder men to shoulder

Those whom fate determines
suffer the splinter
bruise
     of forestry
     rash abrasion
     ragged cut

          Twenty stations haul six grades each
          Fresh hewn fir and poison cedar
          cast-iron hemlock
          lead log vengeful
          at the affront of being sawn

I scarce had arms 'til the summer of '73
       wing rough every sodden stick
       jagged stacks
feed the hunter wheel-legged carry machine

      Alberni Pacific Division
      longest greenchain extant still
      in all the then lumbering world

First shift nightmare by lunch break
drive home barely bear press of
      clutch pedal to foot

          And that gnawing knowing
          before rest could help anything
          back again to the dreadful wood river
          streaming as never to stop

the crush

        tensile authoritative structural beams
        to make lurchmen dream of ease
to fade a summer afternoon
more than a beer after the shift
Escape so far
deep

from   hurtful heat
            back crack

    Fatigue so drunken

        Horror of wet two-by-six
        twenty foot heft
        swarm in sodden stacks

    But the grain was clear
    and the tooth rig shrieked
    delight at blade rip

into pure tree-flesh
Effusion of diamond fleck
    wet confetti
        about the world

    of us millers deaf

        to the outside pleasance
        of poised time
        Champagne with fish roe
        Mountain view and sea
        Pleasing shape
        to put one's hand to

We are
with callus and leather apron
resin souls
amid true boards travelling

Barred by endless log cabinetry
forgotten in dented truck
mortgaged sport coupe
Who through dullness perpetuate
the exiled mind
leaked youth and financed future
4pm pickup tailgate
parking lot tankcar drink
littered ditch glass
lakeside roadway side-glitter
to commemorate passenger girlfriend
of the millionth drop-out conscript

Whose thick dirty digits
in a yearn dizzy
sneak beneath feminine waistband
and by shortness of sight nightly swear
life-long fealty to the chain
running for the builders
proud constructors
hammerists

Conveyor mother mechanical

PORT ALBERNI BLACK LIQUOR

Backyard engine tinker Al and me
    clang whirl clamour town

up from
    some cut-torch fellas atop kraft waste-fuel tank—

air punch

    carport fibre-rattle glass
        valley range reverb crack and back

Lois on the sundeck
    Sounds like the pulp mill

To which Alvin replies
    Sure hope not

She goes in but back ten shakes later
    so-and-so *dead* and so-and-so
    gone to hospital…

The pause

that says we work too near tooth-machine all day
stride ice-chunk river log
gear whine flywheel and oily chain
jerksteer shuddertire gravel fling

    Ignition gases send our dreams aloft

general metal
wax and lube

    …Yep

Regardless

we tune that baby
        get the belt tight

set spark

But damn that ping

ELEPHANT AND TEMPLE

Sawmill comrade Karm Bing
thirty years out of Punjab

> when things were fast and tough on the chain
> would call a cheery
> Yeah right!

smile at my whining

A man who'd seen elephant and temple
> swam holy river
> worship

But absent of mind one near-midnight
making a point
of something

> I felt important to hear
> about Krishna and/or the equinox

rammed a hand
at the end of a two-by-six
jam the stack

Rubber mitt when pulled
> wine bottle pour
> black on the staging floor

> Flee in the aid station night
> dart black&white
> under flood light
> recede shadow

While I shudder and pull lumber
thinking of split finger
how it looks like food

   But then just work
   two spots to tend
   until shift whistle

Never saw Karm again
   warm to remember him

FOREST TOWN SLUMBER

Those who fell awake too late
beneath the toxic blanket

    stagger to heft wood metal paper

numb in the classroom
tote sombre books
wrestle anachronism
fear war and economics

    at any moment
    cover and duck and go away laid off
    from a thousand mill jobs

Who daydream terminal and
sleep off youth
in the phantom mental mist

    seek the big exit

    slur wild in a rebuilt English sedan
    with the boom boom barking doors
    Speak whole lives
    shout violent minds
    force the edge

Skid joyous
in a barren parking lot of snow

POWERSAW LAMENT

Sandpaper time
mill-plane tree
smelt ore
pipeline fluids of the ground

      Teenage workers of the world
      frolic in the affluent effluence
      drive mighty travel machines
      revel hard amid the distractions of growth

      That drug might be too strong
      That car too fast
      Too many beers
      to drink
      to drive
      through a grove

Moloch trunk crash cathedral

And my friend so-and-so
      who defies all opposite forces
      If you listen
      all you hear is no
      to those who live young

Flung in the light above the dashboard
in a final futility
to fall finished
upon polish hood and hard-top

Victim and victor
never old or enlightened by grief

blinded by idea
Not muddled
forsaken
remembered

PICAROON
fibrous asbestos barbs stab minute sacs of being

1)   *Powerplant fireseethe*
       Saw conveyor dust
       Tree furnace perpetual smoke sky
       Friday shutdown Saturday cleanout doomcrew
       Handshovel grip as we crawl into the fire-cooling boiler

Soot vault buccaneer weekend tars awork

       Our picaroons be:
       metal-cap dagger axe wood handle
       clinker mace spike-nose holepunch
       flat-back truncheon

       Cleave ash metal door iron squeak
       plant floor carbon glow hiss pile
       dead sunset ash smolder slump
       Molten pour sidestep

goth inferno cathedral
rise tubewall black
fire water crucible
eternal earth-crypt
fluehole scramble sneeze
heatface cough assault
spade clamber darkness
carbon dangerfog
black hand crawl
glove-melt sole heat

gagflex particle choke
pick dig load wheel
cleanup nail poke floor hole
pickclear airpath
sand nasal build
blackstream nostril rain

2)   *Mesothelioma... mystery of future illness*
     Meso... Japanese soup
     thelioma... kind of zoo creature
     unknown unfeared nothing
     shovelwork lungsacs weep...

     Sledgerollick swing
     mined insulate bushing slam
     mortal mortar fiber rock
     boiler insulate steam pipe
     hot water brake shoe rubble
     clutch pad ceiling tile
     paint corrosion pain

Crawlout victory
Ardent lungful
stoopstand squint
crossplant sunbeam shimmer
Flicker beauty
solar ignition glint
fibrous barb glimmer show

3)   *The doc asks Claustrophobia?*
       machine massive encompasses
       medical whir click capture
       Sedate inducement pill?
       terror outside blood within

       Serpentine silicate molecular spy dagger sick agent

       Magnetic resonance imagine
       tickler chrysotile
       deadfall tomography
       flutter carcinogen rapture

Membrane pleural thicken
millwork memory hum
grindgear mind-din

any and all weeping bounced from the walls
echoed down the hearts of reality and grief
hammered the bulwarks of the great resisters
defeat the supermen's footing

Yearn   regardless   eternal

THE GREAT WANDER...

LAND OF MOUNTAIN & SEA

Down the queued thumbs outside town
sizzle disquiet brain
roadlust

    Garland van-machine
    bearing hair-borne creature
    less material than thought
    wending time and mental space

Natural admix humanity
lysergic warp convergence

    upon the wood-frame seaside metro
    to sit in dingy verse houses
    by the English Bay shore

Bend the pedant
ancient time-held sentiment
rejoice the abandon of temporary poverty
demander of wealth of feeling
eschewer of real estate and bonds
shucked gifted ethics

    Protest together the ridiculous weight
    of the fates of their kin
    mauled by fanged history

    altered velocity
    parenthood of fear
    toiled faces
ground cold by politics
crucial change

to press hope of youth
        back down into pockets
        where hands clench
        fisted

ON THE SUPPOSED ROAD

I

Then off on that seamless ride
wheel and bottle in hand
tire dust flub
in flowered puffer machines

       Starting the engine she had taken me down
       the gentle slope of humanity
       bought a slice of fresh world
       tucked it in my collar

Flying in artless vacuum
fried pigeon in frozen flight
creaking statue limp off
to any direction

       from where it ends
       to find the start
       So answers get questions
       the infinity of flee

       We ranged torn continents
       angry motor below
       eyes and perception fringed crimson
       defying probable justice

To prove our living deaths
against orifice and terminal schedule
stropped bloody against stasis
wrenching the plastic chains

of arranged fates
Fleeing into the near dark
to stumble uncertain
reluctant runners from where

Monday is an immediate Tuesday
Friday is right now
distance exceeds energy
History abrades

and ideas find ground
upon which we settle mad
ride clenched and weeping
down eternal pathway

II

So there it was
us rolling over wet and blue
under-rushing tarmac torrent
You more guide than escapee
Me joying every centimetre behind us

Going from a misfired start
uneasy fortune
The bureaucracy of my brain
surging for interregnum

    And my wide smiling toothsome
    confident knuckles on the wheel
    chuckling back behind
    at something funny or other
    from my paperback lounge

Where I perused deep the profundity
of our lives writ in magnitudinous prose
Reading clips of Kesey and Kerouac
aloud to your willing ear

    and knew in a certain moment
    when I gazed at you gazing out firm
    back toward our cross-country education
    There would come a regret
    and the thing most piteous
    is how soon it came

How we said goodbye
not knowing for sure it was
Then with passing decades knowing
absolute for sure
that those sweet spinning wheels
went together only a road or two
then branched and receded with scarce a wave

    Even before life trouble
    long now wound down
    might have annealed us
    to an alloy of time

ON THAT EON YOU TURNED THIRTY

We heard ice-clink chorus
by the cocktail dozen
in that American bar busy
on a mystery side-road outside
somewhere in Wisconsin

A moment stunned by your hair flung
on a turn to speak
we drank Old Fashioneds and sung your milestone
Did not know when or where life would go
and barely cared

The miles and miles we'd come felt perfect
if only they would stop
as the planet spun on and we stepped
toward the mandate to strive
and establish and proclaim

But synaptic soul desire draws back
to that cherryglass night
as we regaled within chocolate clothing
our savoury hearts sated
on edible freedom

In the spectral warp of happiness
unclutched by wisdom
flowing out the spirit taps of the eternal tavern
atop ethereal woodgrain
a sheen of frozen whiskey

FEDERAL PAROLE OFFICER

SPECIFIC PAIN

Ache of marrow
strive through femur

discomfort sit
with related ones

Strangers but compelled
to ponder every sound

in a crucible of data
Responsibility?

The reason we sit
with mouldering bone

at any given kitchen table
or living room

TV blare and debate
whether dysfunction happened

upon the upholstery of this
inquisition

VANCOUVER BLACK LIQUOR

Had occasion to attend of a drink night

      downtown hotel bar

cross-room observe
parolee amid *et al*
drink-restricted
whose thievy co-drinkers I knew
were not to be with

      Mutual barface interpretation

So no surprise
to the men's room
when I strode
thinking private urination

      standing to at porcelain water flow
      shadow aside sidle up
      otherwise deserted urinebar

said he knew me as a good parole guy
his actual PO not a good guy

      Alisten to this preamble
      Could not ignore
      genital whip-out
      made me look to see
      big hand
      feet

      large

combined total paraphernalia
likely the size of a chicken I'd roasted
not a week ago

      mulled why this was important
      never got an answer but could not help

important notice

      concomitant talk talk
      did not urinate
      No
      talk was what what

      need man to man
      prick in hand
      silence

fraught
the moment for me slightly was

      But he elbow to pass water elbow
      could have taken me

did not

So agreed to quiet I
this occasion
the occasion being had
downtown hotel bar
in company with
whoever was
and whoever should not have been

Most of all

      notwithstanding full comprehension
      this work not mostly pleasant enough
      for universal sunny disposition

disdain bureaucrat myself

      And things morally change from
      upright start
      the longterm law enforcer
      brain to testicle to liver
      through shadowed heart and lung

So when days later
              down the street
      parking underground bullet
found
back-of-head parolee

in gentlemen's urinal agreement

      and because I shook hands with the sentenced led away
      prison floor cold through foot and knee become glass
      nose bleed disinfectant

      and life one must hold firm should someone want it

stood quiet
      as cops asked what was what

WITNESS STATEMENT

given by: THE PASSENGER
at: The Passenger's Residence
Vancouver BC

this date of he can barely remember

Narrative

    I live here and have a telephone
number and a birthdate and Social
Insurance Number

    I have been employed as a law unto myself
by the Solicitor General of Canada
most of my adult life

My office is universally located
I speak regularly urgent
while careening across the city with phone in one hand
steering wheel in other

    At approximately 0950 hours 07 January of a year in the past I was

involved in

    automobile conflict in the 1000 block Station Street
within shadow of the CANADIAN NATIONAL railway station
riding as I was in the front
passenger seat of a 1980 Renault Le Car driven by
my friend Mr Jay

who minutes before had said
upon seeing me recline in my office chair
that I needed coffee
and to follow directions

Get into the car
be the passenger
Ride through the city

Headed for breakfast we thought we'd take an hour or so
to talk ourselves full
partake of the wise choices we'd made
to make crime pay

But enough about that
because
       we proceeded off Main Street and turned east on
       National Avenue
       then right by Station Street

Travelling slow southward
we were struck from behind by a yellow
taxi cab

The unit was Yellow Cab
number eternity
British Columbia license plate
the end
with Transport Canada plate
esoteric identity
and Motor Carrier plate
whatever the case

      At the time we entered
Station Street
from National Avenue

I saw no traffic in either direction which might have been
      impeded
      the least impressed
      interested
      vaguely offended
      by our entrance

As the passenger
I had no opinion about these things ...

Though in fact Mr Jay and I
that day and forever
had
no doubt
      impeded plenty of drivers and others
      by way of our quasi-judicial authority
      and the biases of particular
      foibles
      and personally held prejudices
      and our philosophy of getting through life with minimum scrapes
      The mandate of pleasure
      being our highest order
      beyond even survival
      and preventing our ascension to sainthood ...
      because of course we administered

Temporary Death

Was there ever useful truth
in any punishment thing
all the dragging to lockup?
Was there purpose beyond system
difference past temporary death?

How to toll the lost days?
The dragged weeks and decades
from experienced lives
fate-crazed and hard-lost
to stand handcuffed in shadow?

May he regale in the playful light
of knowing what a fool his passing
made of me
Antics of the bureau
scorned impotent furtive futility

      Committed to artificial solitude
      champions of dangerous pain
      with worse mentalities all the time
      Ready their bodies to the tools
      of mandated procedure

      How to calculate the relative weight
      of every dirty dish
      in the turgid kitchen sinks
      of a multitude taken oblivious
      to the limited time-loss behaviour

The quadriplegic's tears undryable
acid clean my unfilthable soul
which wanders nightly
through jagged memory
of what could save his spine but did not

      About which the salaried
      trudge along the office path
      Wield paper truncheon warrant
      jungle psych report
            Roaring empty info form blank ...

But that's a whole other narrative
which I am sure is not germane to the current

Legal description

of our interrupted morning ritual
of avoiding real work
in a world allowing us leisure at an advantageous age

And overlooked by our spoiled perception
and sense of absurd entitlement
into a state of unconsciousness
unprecedented in human endeavor
but nonetheless practised and taken for granted
by both driver and passenger
in the present circumstances
the magic of our omniscience
interrupted

at the point of physical
collision
our car close to the centre line

poised

to turn left
into a CN station parking space
for breakfast
and the usual gossipy shop-talk

On the northbound side immediately before impact
I observed the witness
Susan
it turns out her name is
of some certified address in town

Young woman
looking beautiful
in our direction

I was
        observing Susan at the time of impact
Who else would I have been observing

I heard no
approach of the taxi
no squeal of tires or sounding of horn
prior to impact
        because Susan

Susan! Susan! Whoa Susan…

        The impact

sent us several metres past the centre line of
Susan Street
I mean
Station Street

Mr Jay brought the car to a stop
set
the handbrake
turned off
the ignition

Glass from the
shattered driver's window spread across his
jacket and clothes

Glass particles also landed in the cuffs of
my passenger trousers

Though uninjured
I found that my hand had flung
with enough force to knock the window
handle knob
off its mounts

but I rued mostly
the temporary loss of my line of sight
knuckles stinging
to our goddess witness
me having well divined much prior to this event
what was most important
to see and remember

But particular to that moment
and making me near forget everything else
was the beauty of the sparkles across our world
Mr Jay and I so garlanded
by more glitter than all the world had to that point
afforded us
In fact we both took long breaths
and in meeting each others' eyes understood
that this perhaps instant
with glorious illumination
and its gauze-filter dreamy aura
might be our life's best (or last)
having survived violent clash
potential for bodily harm
our third-hand stock in trade
served up unexpected and safe
So we might talk about it with smirks
and the full use of reassuring limbs

But
        Subsequent to the accident
I exited the car
forever turning my back
and took
information from the Yellow Cab
License
car number
and other quick particulars

        I then located the witness
Susan
and asked her what she saw

In me
or might
if time allowed
circumstance stood apart
from present necessity
or whatever
As long as she said something

        She stated she saw the Yellow Cab
swift approach our car
        and made sure she remained
remained
in
        observance
observing
because of the taxi's
irresistible
collision
course

Susan Ms I-never-got-her-last-name
was thereby an eye witness to the
Accident

of my not thinking clearly
spinning head
unused to collision impacts
unprepared to do the necessary

Most needed
in times of attraction's urge
sustaining hurt
to memory's paint
dent in the gleaming eye
to remember Susan...

Damage to Mr Jay's vehicle
noted
deep gash on the left
rear side
the driver's door a virtual destroy
not operable as we drove away later

Taxi
sustained limited marks
the chrome
broken signal lens

Immediately Driver Jay
complained of stiffness
I observed that he could be shaken
having like me
taken the major force of systemic coercion
autonomic prison door clang
distant heartfelt despair

to make stone walls weep
amid paperwork anesthesia
for most of our adult lives
and cumulative toll
to dwarf the effects
of the impact on his side of the
car

      At the time of the accident
both driver and myself
were wearing lap and shoulder belts
and were in no mind to follow up
on incarcerative work
or any productive public representation

      I had not consumed any
      drug
      or alcohol in the day

But certainly intended
by night

And for sure seemed
lost
intoxicate
jubilant at ourselves and willing...

      Jay and I motored on
      and would over the years come to at least consider our fellow man
      to

      All hail the government office musician
      bureaucrat novelist
      stenograph ballerina
      file cabinet actor
      and the system analytic performance artists

Who secrete themselves amid the memos
and softhead algorithms

And emerge nightly
having funded their search
underwritten national life

Financed the thought

that by sheer emergence

keeps us riding and riding

I HAVE READ THE ABOVE TOO-MANY PAGE REPORT AND
BELIEVE IT TO BE
TRUE

Signed

The Passenger

ALCATRAZIM

Yeah I once used a southwest cell
with a Golden Gate view
and I wish that Jew landlord
got got by Hitler
And I don't care a damn
that you you softie social worker
once walked the tiers
pretended to eat in the mess hall
with the screws and the gangsters and the pervs

They were all joints in them days
They're all joints now
It's all just pain to me you hear?
I hate you for making me remember
Why you want to know about this stuff anyway?
Some kinda morbidity of the soul?
Dirty interest in other people's badness?

So you walked around North Beach with a white suit on
went to City Lights and bought a book
strolled Chinatown in a sport jacket
The one you're wearin now and it looks sad

Drank in the bars and spoke to cheap women
pretended you had cool
Took them to the Legion of Honour Museum
place I read about one time in a brochure
picture of The Thinker thinkin in the garden
Yeah right and never comin ta any conclusion
so put-on even Row-din couldn't help ya

And even willing women couldn't jolt off the stupid
from your determined suckhole face
that doesn't know dick all
because you were never there you fraud
San Francisco does not know you
Not even the hookers and stripper trash
would let you tie their shoes or tell what time it is

What did you ever do but tourist?
Can you tell that kike miser to back off my back?
Give me more time to get up the rent?
Get me in a place to live with whiskey and swearin
Do something anything that justifies your paycheque
from taxes I would've paid if I went straight

And don't think I don't think about it
going back to the pistol and the car
Just 'cause I'm old enough to done time with Karpis
handed chow to Bob Stroud and heard his sick mouth
walked that exercise yard where they do all them movies

Don't dream I wouldn't dream of givin it to somebody
An old man just gets meaner is what I've found
so don't get all sentimental on me
Nothing spiritual about a joint
Older it gets the meaner it gets
the more I'd like to plug somebody right now
So unless you're comin with me
get outta the way

ATTRACTIONS...

Though your tremolo heart may be
        kicked black
miracle eye-glint will
capture
wordless jail men

tame and retrain their reflected
        inner grime
supply sooty handhold
to all
but your own

cinderizing spell to unclasp the million
        cell doors
and burn penitentiaries
to the
odious rooftop

Dream of gambling machines bong bing but hot
for the change girl who is young but old
see us in a Reno bed months later
her old man getting out of the joint...

Dance of strict action-movie business

Lady of the pages
litter of words
margin
prefix and suffix
in her hair

Her eyes
the future
the truth
of our inventions

Your spins
make my head
stand still

remember
the visual whirl
mental dervish

through my eyes
a lilt-crazy
dancer laugh

in my empty room
torque flighty damage
to my darkness

Mystery I said
in your face
craved and lost

but then crawled across my head
bit my ears
for pain and comprehension

my hair in sparks
I cannot run
cannot walk unless you unplug me

There it is
that look
of melting chickens
awaiting

Is it red in your hair?
Am I thinking
beyond sight
to see what I can't?

So bright when you
speak
the picture
is not necessary

Stir me brain downward
organic intelligence being

Your slated poise of face
my ticking clock

Loud enough to open those
brown historical eyes

your silence is
detention

I exist in expectation
to hear electric waves
of your face
and the way your head tilts
when it
thinks

So there they are
eyes
drinking
me
and the face
drawing
hand
reach
down the front of me
and tease
render
all
heart
stomach
all
I mean all

In a boxing ring
with the biggest
gloves

never use them

Gaze placid at the lacing up

The count is ten
please get off my heart

If what's wrong
comes from
something near my
pituitary gland
I'll have it excised
pickled
in polski ogorki brine

If it's environmental
I'll climb a mountain
somewhere
though I'm afraid
of heights

Either way I come to you
parts missing

Whoa
yes
with the snow falling
the quiet
roaring calm
in our heads
the embrace
all there
the hug
down to the cells
the sinew
laughter and happiness
the thrill
melted
as
whipped cream
on baked potato
the wrong stuff
but
yes

You are your cats
gray
shy
under the bed
near imagined

Then of course there's the
black
with spots
bolts for the hallway
every chance

Does a magic sylph
wisp an unconscious face

sleep so complete
her splendour leaves an idle heart

Shadow
the way your face
leans
toward me
this quiet place we talk

The words
charm
tinkle and speak
make the dark
important

Flicker image interminable
World War Two

Corpses piled
Nazis in uniform

Lean down to say
love is fatal

Though evidence suggests
No love is worse

Just wait
I'm thinking about you
on a bus to somewhere
and me
drinking
scowling at the wall

It doesn't matter
I never see you again
we die
you hate me
time keeps us apart

I touch you
head to head
sweet melting
in the back of someone's car
and I flee now
goods finely stowed

As I try to collect the hours
I am a stopped man
striding aside you
and your sweater
only goes
partway down

you
sweetly
ask me to make it
go
all the way

With my hands
I trace your
self
and stop breath
hope
for life
in your clothing

Yes
Dear I know
Death may come
in your wink
As my joy flowers upon your every nuance
teasing my tenuous hold upon sanity
as I reach with my eyes and my fingers to your core

I ask you questions
of family
and life
because when you
do
finally
kill me
I'll need to know the source
of the blade
the tearing bullet
that blanks
my diminishing
care
and breath

Of course
I shouldn't pine
crave
sacrifice myself
upon the desire
to touch
your fingernail
or taste the air
after you've passed
through the sundry crowd
and brave furious wind
which announces you

I wonder if from
space
in the eyes of the
satellite
when I bent
on the dampened seawall enfolding you
and kissed carefully
the back of your neck

Did it look like
love
or
murder?

I can be staggered
by the beauty
of solitary construction sites
towers
with lights and rubble
and lonely snow
upon trailers
and concrete
because I know
that you
have flakes of ice on your sweater
and I am there
getting wet
too

From my vulnerable sides
front and back
Valkyries scream
desperate men drive through town
hatred in their teeth
but I am strung
with guilt and weariness
and bleeding from my eyes
and itching in the brain
wondering
through doubt and sadness
all I can think of
all that is there
is the way your body
moves
as it moves
away
through the jean-jackets and bargain-wear

Your gentle step narcotizes me
When you see my eyes I'm safe
Your hair is a nest I want to infest
You thrill me with competence
I like the look of your fingers
Your quietness rests in beautiful music
I envy the words you read
Your house
your cat

What is it? This mystery that
    slurs your face to me
    Makes my life a boiling water

    Do I look inside me? For answers or clues
    some comforting truth
    a platitude I can believe in and hold to my chest

    Can I look inside you?
    Burning eyes blind and singeing soul

    What will we do? To save ourselves the heat
    and torture. Or are we cursed
    unlucky farmers
    to work the soil and harvest only stones.

SOMME WHEAT FIELD...ALL OUR WARS

YES NORTHERN CANADA VIETNAM

(DICHLORODIPHENYLTRICHLOROETHANE...MESOTHELIOMA)

Yes I wore the uniform and got sent north
Mosquito-pock out-lie region

Churchill Manitoba

Somebody else's
 fly-clog summer lake playground
 Whilst instructing military teens to paddle canoe
a device
perhaps justly relegated to
comedy status

  but romantic nonetheless for its marriage of the
  sensuous and drowned

That was the year I got doused with DDT
nineteen seventy-one in clouds of

unknown

But it was
 the first time missing a girl
 and what a girl she was
Landmark
sexual demarcation in a
bug-craze miasma

  but romantic to disappear energy into that
  mystery nether region

So there I marched in the swat-face sub-Arctic
and later on shovelling boilers got a couple of
asbestos lungs

in the massed
          West Coast lumber machine

boredom
          to writhe nails out of petrified wood
bug bite
scratch cough industry...

          though preferred

yes
          to a
          greening spot

yes

          in Asian jungle

LOOK BOTH WAYS

A car hit me aglance
askance

side mirror fling perilous
loose part

on rhythmic tap tap
pavement

Took my arm to dance
circular

compulsory revolve
as if to

remind all who stride
astride

Watch the hell out because
there is

art to do or such whatever
activity

it is that keeps you
upright

GOIN' DOWN THE ROAD ODE TO DOUG MCGRATH

Pete
if ever the bacon did not fry
under Joey's
                    purdy low
heat

When cars won't start

        because they're beaters
        clunked in from neighbours' yards
        Bail wire coalescence of amateur

                            nationality

Chug suds-cloud bottle intoxicate
for purpose of further relax
amid the general recline

        Yes I see the road before us
        your fist upon the knuckled steer

                        Look back

smilesome and damned

ANTICIPATED RESULTS

Hanging with boozers is fun maybe
     pathetically curious
         anthropologically interesting

    But sooner than later you get ignored and become
obscure

    Do badly at work and never get
promoted

    Get cancer whether you smoke
or not
    Forget you drink to forget you're drinking
to forget

    Philosophize but not say
anything

    Live long but never
grow up

Run out of money
Run out of time

MOTHER DREAMS IN GERMAN

Snowflat cruel growlands abrade
immigrant face
        bully wind wreathe

        Landscape to drive grain back into the soil
        Shiver plague and pang stomach silence haunt

Nicht

All she can remember is winter
a snow sky merciless
Shudder

I would never go back there

        Schoolroom. Lard bread. Granite look of Teacher
        bundle-rub to fight a little girl's frostbite

Nicht

Wire jolt removes her favourite horse
too near a lightning-struck fence

        Does sanguine prairie girl sense thus
        determine true what will be and what not?

Nicht... Ich würde nie never never

Sick calf maundering mother's coat
Locust grain voracious gopher destiny

        Hardscrabble childhood frayed shoelace
        Hands in frosted pain mitts

Nicht

        Ach ach!

Nicht

Workthick digits on rock-pick hands
If one must go one must go

        Dustwhorl spirit sweep *nein*
        cloud tower caution *nein nein*

        Würde nie… nicht

CLASSROOM 1942

From a reading chair on 21st Century Avenue
rooftop to glass row

      Vancouver Tech High School

son of a World War Two morning lad listen
note the persistent

      heritage gears
grandfather
      time engine bootstomp echo

Get up, boy! You're hired down at the shipyards...

Who stood
ready

      and later on felt right to thoughtfully flee
      try breathe the free air
      See and hear and fight

the stolen chance to see out

      And who frighted at the burble inside
      that made this troubled man
      whose proud false teeth
      frown
      rage

      made the only grief
      to make a son's heart weep

Years of not good enough
to assuage a fine deprivation
curse and misinterpret
        by silence and alcohol

In the house with punishment windows
        no lounge place to contemplate the strained present
        moist want of learning's return

Anger wrings to work and do
Tearburn
pierce the judgment hand

ED

You said you never went in for that
That sentimental stuff
That makes you soft in the chest
That claims your brain and
You had me convinced you'd never do anything
To cause me tenderness
As we drank in the kitchen

Then you died
Ed
After taking it full on
Like a man
Never soft
I held you and carried you where you needed to go
And then you were gone
Wordless and tough

So I was struck down
Punched in the heart
Not daring a sound

A week later riding a bicycle
car whiffed so close
I still shudder the bristling scalp

Scratches on the paint
water bottle in the hands
of a back seat girl

The presence of ghosts and cold

And knew I'd never get drunk enough that day next day ever
to forget about it

I dreamt you and me drinking in the kitchen
I asked what the hell you were doing drinking in the kitchen with me
Looked sad at me and said soft *I guess you don't know*
Don't know what?
Don't know you're dead
Aw shit that car...
... Killed you
and now you're here

Only your words and the care in your face
your words soft as I'd never known
A life regret not looking into your eyes
Raspy throat and chest of loneliness
was what I was left with
once and again
like a time after that and a time after that
tender in the soul
For you
who left a gap
And me now too
who dead in a dream
felt better than now
and yearns for another drink
in the kitchen with you
Ed

      All my souls black as my stare
      Fatal diamond dagger cold as love lost

THE SOMME WHEAT FIELD

ALBERT, PICARDIE, FRANCE, MAY 1989

The wind does not answer questions
It's just cold

Perhaps there was never a time
we knew what this wheat field meant

The day I was born the men here had been
thirty-five years   in this wheat field

I am thirty-five now
older than most of them

I walk that cold dirt path
suspicious pieces of underfoot metal

The wind has power here
It'll get worse when the last of them come out

from their old-age places
and return

Quite soon now there will be a full complement
in this wheat field

Maybe then with all their hearts together
They'll be able to reason it out

The wind does not answer questions
It's just cold

But through the laden grime and up through the feet
visceral to the mind
lives are played

as by a spirit
memory made animate
by the wind
by the cold

By the voices

who reach but are glad
they do not reach

Do I hear time or terror?

They writhe to understand
hold still here in staring query
a world which invented their permanent residence
in mud and seedling grain

After all what were they

cherished sucklings?

lone branch
against leaden sky?

crows
cawing
nightward
at flagging day?

What are they for?
Does Victory save them?

*   *   *

Boys were boys no more
    faces not shiny coins...

              I will win this war for you

              I'll carry the day

But

    there will be
              shards
    raw skin
    sad   seep

Amid the mistaken society of war
    Under the crawling depth of hunger

    In the limousine window of whoredom...

whoever thought a bus stop
    would be a flak zone?

    Swing punch-glow drunkards
    milltown angry kick blow
    burst away all

*   *   *

...And who will forget brave Charlie Burnett? His Irish cigarette
    onehand roll skill
at age 82 tremulous in his small Victoria house

Learned that at the front
    Twenty years old I was

    tobacco history
    mudded boot trench-huddle near Mons
    while the first 1914 shots

flew—fade...

... And sailor John Webster's social work soul on the Murmansk run
    stoic and jokey
    at a freeze death
    or corvette drown

            The only WWII vet around
            who'd journeyed LSD and it was the best thing
            in the world
            with nary a navy regret and inquiry toward
    all things

    human

    who when asked once what was it like to lose interest in
girls
answered at 75

    Let you know if it happens...

... And Stalag-bound Merv Davis flutters out the broken middle of their
    halved Halifax
        splinter Messerschmitt scream
            not-dropped bombs first to hit

Some of us didn't get out... over coffee and talk about
how other humans can be saved by parachute of
compassion
patience and knowledge that things can be a Luft III
damn sight worse

if we don't navigate together at least a little

Calm of a lifelong Savary Island summer to assuage a
rage hurt heart...

... And pre-law Harry Rankin march Seaforth o'er Burrard Bridge
en route to Italy blood slog
ancient masonry rubble

Ortona

the Vimy of Canada's WW II and unsung
except for counsel's admonition that the men of that era
were heroes of a particular sort

Whose address to the bullet
whizz above
instruction to the jury
lifelong
never concede...

... And addled Londoner Archie Rowell's rave of demons
curse the flak flak
metal terror rain that at age 85
veteran of all the wars in a closet village street
in peaceful eastcoast Vancouver Island

meted careful jawbreaker and penny-fraction sour
No matter he lost everything

    in July 1965 he was gone and us schoolkids

oblivious to time and past
    knew nothing
        jawbreakers and sours all...

... And everybody's pal Cas Anderson of the cutaway face
    sidespeak mumble friendly talk
only man I ever saw eat pure beef fat and make it look yummy

Who on his gather of milk on the Coombs countryside
    spoke of the morning fusillade
      We'd fire over there and hide

the Germans would shoot back...

... And listen to stiff-walk Private Joe Clegg talk snowball fight
    giddy panic blood charge
    Polderland thrill
    Normandy savage
            We met these SS crazies
    hard helmet
Had to shoot 'em in the face
    they kept comin' 'cause they thought we were low class

... And livid Walter Bergmann who'd never been in such shape
        from cross-field rifle and grenade
        drill
                that saved his life

        those weeks near Caen

                so he could be the brave
                obsessed teacher of eager elementary school
        boys enthrall ...

... And stealth Norman Parisien elite killman Cree huntbreed
        in a thousand Legion appearances swept
                ranks of women in gliding waltzstep
                        foot-flight to dazzle and suppress

                back of mind

Stalk Roman wine-grove Nazi prey
odd racial no doubt terror to quizzical Aryan tribe ...

... And why does 3rd Medium Gunner Lod Gardner in his living assist
        whiskey life at 96 still hear 5-inch blast
        and cringe at silverware clash?

Who'd rather joke
        at AWOL jaunts down London
                than the truck rumble March '45 through flame
                        coming up on citizen Dutch-fired Emden ...

... And everybody likes tankman Chris Conway whose town Scottish fool
        with humour and light
        no one outdid

ever memory held off char metal-clad remains

        Or the scorn muddied fellows afoot from Market Garden
        dark and sore and few
due they thought
        to Armour's reluctance

        to engage...

... And of course locked up Percival Arlington of the infantry escape corps
        walk scout far from officerdom as a fella can
        and not get nabbed by Jerry

But when taken as he was six times *They were kinda hoit-toit fellas*
                    didn't know about dirty fightin'
                    didn't know I grew up in

    East Van ...

... And feist-short Jack Ashbridge   Survival
        by sheer sneer at all who
        pretend
        to think a man quivers just because Death
        be at hand...

... And so to Sergeant Bert James that loving man's jovial frown
        six years gone of his life in England
        Belgium
        Germany

Walk aside khaki mates with Bren in hand and sleep terror
for my aunt to shake awake

Me

    the one in the family who ever heard him
    speak
    You know I saw it fly like fire hose
        Shoot
cross the street...

And stop my talk
    start my listen
        But there wasn't more Uncle would say

and now he's marched off with the others...

            *   *   *

Does tomorrow exist?

        for us
            Think
    and suffer over time that might not be
        when our bright
    happiness
    could make flower grow from rock

Why should we love? If just miserable mystery
    it brings. Mean as poisoned food
    holding life
    while it burns
        the heart away

    Beauty is irrelevant amid the mistaken society of war

    Beware the assumption of grace
        comely through the ages

for faces might weep
     out a boxcar door
          as time dines joyous
            on us all

Fix them in your mind
          why do they not play?

          *   *   *

I am of the future now
older than all of them
and it is cold to walk this dirt path
There are suspicious pieces of metal

The wind has power here and it is
worse now the last of them have come out from
their old-age places

There is a full complement
in this wheat field

Maybe now
with their hearts together
they will have reasoned it out

The wind does not answer any questions
It's just cold

Vancouver, British Columbia, June 2013

CREDITS

"Powersaw Elegy" appeared in *Alive at the Centre*, Pacific Poetry Project, Ooligan Press, University of Oregon, 2013.

"Land of Mountain and Sea" appeared in *subTerrain* #59, Vancouver 125 special edition, 2012.

"Chain Canticle," "Everybody," "Tough" and "Root Beer" were broadcast on the November 9, 2011, edition of *Wax Poetic*, Vancouver Co-op Radio.

"Forest Town Slumber" and "Powersaw Elegy" were performed as part of the Mashed Poetics reading series, Vancouver, BC, 2011.

The author of seven books of fiction and veteran of a two-decade career with the Correctional Service of Canada, DENNIS E. BOLEN is also an editor, teacher, journalist and now poet. He holds a BA from the University of Victoria and an MFA from the University of British Columbia, and he taught creative writing at UBC from 1995 to 1997.

dennisbolen.com